I0202366

Guilt and Life

ADRIAN ARMANCA

Guilt and Life

DEDICATION

Aaron and Hannah.

Guilt and Life

CONTENTS

Guilt and Life

ACKNOWLEDGMENTS

Thanks to my sweetest critics,
Loolee and Poopy.

Guilt and Life

Guilt and Life

Downunder

There is a land south of the world,

Red hot like fire, glazed with gold.

I stepped on it, at my first touch,

The vibe, the magic grasped me tight.

A land where time has never been

Where words like old means only new

A land where future has no past

Where everything is there to last.

Where humans aren't nature's choice

Where trees and rivers come in first

Only the strong that could live on

Were here since rock was running hot.

Things have changed, life has moved on,

There were a few who want them gone

Yet, as the first ones always say

We're not just here, we're here to stay.

They have adopted some of us,

The ones who put the nature first

The ones who give not only take

Soft at heart yet hard to break.

November 2019

Rainbow

The light has split in seven ways

Some prefer the red or green

Others simply love the sixth

Yet no one ever likes the greys.

The orange means a deal for few

For others yellow says a lot

Violet always brings a thought

Yet most of them will run from blue.

Mixing in between the worlds

The other rainbow made its way.

The old wants something cruel to say

Yet never learned to use the words.

November 2019

Night

Windows covered with fire

Soon a memory of the horizon,

Faces in the mirror lost their light

Through opened doors came in "the midnight"

We spoke, we played, we just enjoyed

We swapped, we gave, we trade-exchange

What's mine it's yours, you have me all

Through all this couldn't see the flaw.

The time has faded with the dark

On our infinite walk in the park.

A light from the sky, rain fall

Way back turned to be ephemeral.

They called to say I'm late

And asking if I'm with my date.

A month has passed, nobody knew

That her and me we went askew.

November 2019

Awaken

Ring, it's early and he's up

Somehow, he waited for this

He wished all night for his morning cup

He wished for the first drag, sweet bliss.

Held tight in the dark blue light

A bashful, shapeless creature appeared.

Late, he botched the early start

Planned to keep him safe and spared.

No vision, no future, just an end

No dreams, all lost with the first breath.

That's the life with turn and bend

Goes by, no sight, just shadow. Stealth.

November 2019

Time to...

Give me more lashes, don't take my time

The only thing that keeps me alive

Freedom is my lifelong gift

Given to me by random pick.

I had the chance to change the world

I had a dream to fix its mould,

Then time has put his dirty paws

Until was sure to keep its course.

All my changing dreams are gone

And left behind an empty goal,

There is a saying from the old

Don't try to change or move the world.

December 2019

Valkstone

Passing through the metal gates

A bunch of pupils with their mates,

I was so small between them all

Teachers were giants, strong and tall.

They split us into separate groups

Small little armies, only cute,

The giants I told you about

Became so sweet and big at heart.

The years went by, I'm still a child

Only much taller, a different kind

Smarter, brighter with respect

For the giants and the rest.

This is about the Valkstone school

Where I learned to use the tool

The most important out of all

Called "brain", most powerful yet small.

December 2019

Greeks

Standing in between the seas

A blessed and precious land of Greece

From Knossos all the way to north

Or Athos to the land of Rhodes.

It takes ten days or even more

To count the years since they were born

The people from the famous books

Written by Homer about the Greeks.

Some say the sculptured, polished world

Has started from this mythic realm,

Paintings, theatre, books and statues

Philosophy and mathematics.

From Pella, just a dot on land,

Raised with the sword into his hand,

Alexander called the Great

For his stature and his strength.

His tutor was Aristotle

Who taught him all about the world,

He commanded mobs and army

From the Athens to New Delhi.

The history has just begun

With modern Greeks taking the land,

The waters conquered with their boats,

The skies with Zeus and his Gods.

December 2019

Final Line

There is a line you shouldn't cross

Or bet on it who gets there first,

Live your day like it is your last

Once, at the end, you will be right.

When future it's not bright ahead

Step back a little, take a break.

The healing will be truly short

Not one day long, but half at most.

You'll find a reason to wake up

Even knowing it is your last

To smell the roses, see the light

And wish that one day you'll be back.

Obey the Gods or trust the nature

Both ways have the same destination

At six feet under or below

With hope you will morph into fuel.

December 2019

Shag

Bringing life into this world,

Terrible, ugly, and cold,

Would be a sin if you believe

Or a mistake if you are real.

The instinct couldn't be suppressed,

Same one that lets you procreate.

We even change its name for glamour,

From now it's "sex", a word with fervour.

There are no feelings in the act

Just a reciprocating fact,

Pushing in and sliding out,

Like Carnot cycle of a truck.

Melange of liquids, juices, sweating,

Towards the end of act called "mating",

One can't say no, it's all go, go

Until the vessels overflow.

December 2019

Narcis

He sees the world through a long cone

The other end, not the one small,

He hears what only wants to hear

Always about him, words that smear.

He feels that all belongs to him

The trees, the sunset, human beings,

But all he wants is to admire

His shapeless face into a mirror.

He feeds on other's suffering

Their tears, his only comforting,

He wouldn't take "no" as response

He'll crush you if he hears a curse.

I, Mine, Me plus superlatives

Will always come between his lips,

Demeaning words to make us small

To put him up on pedestal.

December 2019

Time

Quarter past Mesozoic,

Gong will beat Palaeozoic,

Proterozoic soon will come,

In short time will be Hadean.

Times one, times ten, times millions

Hours, days or even years,

Will disappear like never been

Humans, forgotten like a dream.

The rocks will always turn around

There will be light but won't be sound,

Days will be years, nights last for months

Will be just planets, no more Earths.

Life's colours like the greens and blues

Where else you'll find in Universe?

The life on Earth, story, or legend

For whom if there's no one to listen?

The final's close, there's nothing left

Only a bunch of rocks and dust,

The wind has blown away last traces

Of, once majestic, human species.

December 2019

Solange

A tiny slope towards the edge

The Sun has chosen to emerge,

Has made the vortex to imbibe

The finest from the other side.

Can't see the beauty only size,

Class and style are in disguise,

We thought is black with horns and tail,

It's opposite but still named "devil".

We made a pact with the above

To let him feed from our barn,

Until the time to give away

Our bruised souls to his envoy.

His name is Solange and was sent

By mighty devil from the east,

Who plays with our world the games,

Which sometime loses, mostly gains.

Who said he's small and less evolved?

He reproduced a massive herd!

Who could encircle fifty times,

The earth, holding each other's hands.

Why Solange, why not Un or Bhang?

Why Latin, why not eastern tang?

Because false, fake, theft and deceit

Comes easier when you're a cheat.

December 2019

Memories

To have them, you had to be living

Not be alive or just surviving,

Memories, tools from the past

Which help us live up till the last.

Where are they going when they're lost?

Untold or simply just forgot,

Will they ever return to us?

When time is just a hopeless curse?

Once they are gone, they're gone forever

Don't even try to find the answer,

The time will ditch you once again

Until your life goes down the drain.

December 2019

Deep Rest

A strong feeling is creeping in

Closed, locked, shut, terrifying,

The only walls are of a sphere

Sunken in a deep, dark sea.

Giving up now looks so sweet

When only exit is defeat,

Lost all your hope, your god is dead

While hearing voices in your head.

Go to sleep, never come back

Dream about the things you lack,

Like freedom, wind, the sound of nature

At times forgets that you're its creature.

December 2019

Fate

We only had the sense of space

Then we invented something fierce,

It has a dozen ways to measure

And it's abstract yet part of nature.

We think of it only so seldom

When days are grey and full of boredom,

The rest of them are just tick tock

Keeps its pace for us to track.

We're angry when it goes too slow

We're happy when it's easy flow,

But then we realise too late

It's not just time, it is your fate.

December 2019

Cruel

She lures you in with her allure

Her lips are sweet, her eyes are pure,

Nothing there to fear just yet

Until you walk into her net.

There're two of them, they lay you down

Cover you up until you're bound,

It's like a tandem kind of act

With harmony, whisper, and tact.

She starts by opening your mouth

Puts toy like objects in words' path,

Sunglasses covers your whole face

You're nothing special, just a case.

I had real feelings not a dream

Until her needle pinched my skin,

She snatched them all with just a touch

The serum flowing in a rush.

She tapped my face softly and tender

Asking if I feel her finger,

I felt nothing only her scent

Coming from her luscious hand.

Metal clacking, lots of motion

Grinding bits at high rotation,

All prepared, ready to go

To penetrate through teeth and bone.

An hour later I was done

Exhausted, toothless, feeling down,

My speech reduced to mumbling

The putrid smell still lingering.

I said goodbye with just a glance

Still trying to escape the trance,

With hope to never re-enact

The torture from below the light.

January 2020

Give and Take

Lost in thoughts, the guilt prevailed

It showed him life's a privilege,

The ones unborn, will they receive

The priceless, precious gift "to live"?

Where will they go if stuck in space?

Or in some place without a trace?

What if they're not scribed on the list?

What if for them there is no gift?

As cynical as we can be,

We all will have to pay the fee

To pass through time and leave a sign

Barely acknowledged when you're gone.

Ha, ha, he sits and laughs at us,

Eager and keen to take our breath,

To say the words that feed his soul,

"Your time has come, it's time to go".

Unborn and waiting in the line,

Watching him laugh with eyes that shine,

And show his finger to the next

Followed by new one as pretext.

We had enough fear and control,

You keep your gift, just take it all!

We shouldn't live knowing we're next

By name and written as a text!

There are no gods or some creators

Who sit and laugh while giving orders,

They're all just stories in our head

Read to us kids when gone to bed.

February 2020

Scared

Hurt and fragile, scared to blink

Shut my thoughts, try not to think,

Famous seven has arrived,

Year who bought us to an end

Seven years planning the future

Seven years of tears and torture,

Emotions with a violent tone

Struck me through my skin and bone.

Morning came with light and buzz

The room was blurry, filled with fuzz,

I couldn't see two steps ahead,

The only safe place was my bed.

An island with secluded caves

A country town in Middle West,

My thoughts were flying to these places

To run away from all their faces.

They said "remain, let times go by"

"You will forget, others will come",

I chased them all with hurtful words

While throwing knives, arrows, and
swords.

They didn't lie, they spoke the truth,

Hard times had made me cold, aloof,

The past times faded, weeds have grown,

No memories to fill the void.

I locked it up and threw the key

No one could reach nor hear or see,

Buried deep in cold and darkness

My once vivacious soul, now lifeless.

March 2020

Paranoia

Frightening shadow

Afraid of the light

Hidden below

Away from sight.

A muffling sound

Travelled through boards

Leaving behind

A night filled with thoughts.

Thoughts of more darkness

Where end is near by

Asleep, yet so conscious

And dreaming to die.

I hoped he won't find

The door to my world

Thoughts in my mind

Tortured my soul.

I knew it was morning

Though light didn't shine

A long, muted squeaking

This time it was mine.

April 2020

Petty Killers

A wailing din covered the land,

Then suddenly a crying sound,

Made you forget that there's no god

Made you forget that life's a fraud.

A sweet sound of a crying violin

Submerged in sorrow, soaked with pain,

Has told the story in few notes

The story of a million words.

Frozen hearts melting away

Voided places filled with joy,

Hope still nowhere to be seen

As for love? Who else was keen?

The sudden wind has changed its way,

The wailing din came back to stay,

The melted hearts all froze again,

The short-lived joy was all in vain.

The blast before the fiddle ended

Was of a bomb who has just landed,

The gift of life it was returned

Joy giving talent shortly trailed.

Old sound of death refilled the valley

The furnace blow burning the bodies,

White beams of light lifting the souls

Alas, just rays piercing the clouds.

Watching us with vapid eyes,

Cruel, bony face that terrifies,

Tall, blond, named Gunter like his father,

From different camp, same petty killer.

Barbaric thoughts run through his brain

Thinking he's god, no more a swine,

His mug was lit with witless joy

At blasting sight who killed that boy.

He paid back after forty years

Trying to escape his fears,

Hiding in a deep dark sty

With two blonde piglets and a sow.

May 2020

Virus Games

He made a bid to rule the world

Not knowing what it will unfold,

They say it's little like a gnome,

And has an extra chromosome.

●

They say he plays with human genes

Injecting them in monkey's brains,

We know it's further from the truth

But there's no other left to choose.

His phallic size is of a pin,

His head is flat, his lips are thin,

The tongue is wide, teeth like a fork,

They say he belches like a pork.

They say he doesn't eat just rats

Sometimes for breakfast feeds on bats,

Do we believe in all these tales?

Or trust the word that truth prevails?

May 2020

Transcendent

They heard a faded, feeble sound

The source of it couldn't be found,

Was of a dog, a goat or rodent

Loud just enough to make it noticed.

The day has brought a din and noises

People talking, screams, yells, voices

The feeble sound was all forgotten

Until the day has dropped its curtain.

Again, they heard it thundering

Men with their torches rummaging,

The growl was louder, cleaner, deeper

The screech, then howl made it grimmer.

A farrago of myths and stories

Creep them up with fears and worries

Meagre faces, yellow glowing

Ominous voices, constant roaring.

Stewing apprehensive thoughts

Surmised to stories without doubts

The priest has told them is the end

Apocalyptic times attained.

An opened fracture through the ground

Followed a crepitating sound

Exposed the entrails of the earth

An image seemingly of death.

A reek of sulphur mixed with bowels

Reaching through every mortal's nostrils

Came through the cracking fractured
ground

A textured haze with whooshing sound.

There's nothing mystical about

A sewage pipe that's blowing up

Nothing transcendent of the scent

Coming from someone's excrement.

July 2020

Guilt and Life

ABOUT THE AUTHOR

Adrian Armanca, the author behind Guilt and Life.
Well-travelled, engineer, a user of the human condition.
Witnessed globalization, injustice, freedom, tyranny,
peace, not war, communism, democracy, gentle and
violent emotions, nihilism, cynicism.
From the Transylvanian city of Cluj Napoca in the
heart of Romania.